# INTO THE AMAZON

ONE LOST WORLD | THIRTY MEN | SEVEN MYSTERIES

by Douglas W. Phillips

Vision Forum Ministries

First Printing


*"Where there is no vision, the people perish."*

Vision Forum Ministries
4719 Blanco Rd., San Antonio, Texas 78212
1-800-440-0022
www.visionforum.org

ISBN: 978-1-9374600-0-6

Cover Design by Austin Collins
Typography by Justin Turley

Printed in the United States of America

## Other Curriculum Sets *from* Vision Forum

*WWII: D-Day and the Providence of God*

*The Young Ladies' Study Course for Proper Writing*

*Biblical Economics: A Complete Study Course*

*Law & Government: An Introductory Study Course*

*The History of Christianity and Western Civilization*

*The History of the World Collection*

# Table of Contents

# INTO THE AMAZON

ONE LOST WORLD | THIRTY MEN | SEVEN MYSTERIES

Episode 1

# The Mystery of the Meaning of the Amazon

On the third day, God created trees. From trees he gave man fruit, oxygen, and building materials—the very stuff of life for man's dominion of the earth. More than 6,000 years after creation, trees remain a staple of the earth's ecosystem—a living testimony to the wisdom of the Creator. And nowhere on earth are trees more plenteous than in the Amazon rainforest.

With more than 1.4 billion acres of rainforest, and an estimated 400 trees per acre, there are more than half a trillion trees in the Amazon. And they replenish at a remarkable speed. It takes only 40 years for these trees to sprout and grow to 100 feet in height.

Amazonia is a world of secret tribes and of lost civilizations. It is a world that has tempted many explorers and adventurers to brave death by insect, arrow, and man-eating creatures, and to forsake civilization in search of conquest, gold, and the answers to ancient mysteries.

The diversity of creation in the Amazon is simply astounding. With more than 2.5 million species of insects, at least 40,000 species of plants, and thousands of species of mammals, reptiles, and birds, the Amazon is home to the largest collection of plants and animals on planet Earth.

But the Amazon is not without controversy. Her future on earth, and man's relationship with her, are just two of those controversies. More than anything, the Amazon is at the epicenter of a great religious conflict—a war between two competing worldviews: those who worship the Creator, and those who insist on worshipping the creation. This is the story of the Amazon in the twenty-first century.

Watch "The Mystery of the Meaning of the Amazon", and then answer the following study questions to document what you learned.

# Study Questions

1. Genesis 2 introduces us to the first man, who was commissioned to perform taxonomical classification on animal species, to tend a garden, and to utilize certain trees for his benefit while not eating of the tree of the "knowledge of god and evil." Can you think of other examples of the importance of taxonomy and stewardship over gardens in the Bible? Can you find examples in Scripture of how the Lord uses trees to teach spiritual lessons?

2. Can you think of five ways in which the Amazon rainforest is different from the Garden of Eden?

3. How big is the Amazon rainforest? How much fresh water flows through the Amazon? How many trees are there in the Amazon?

4. The biblical doctrine of dominion is rooted in the commission of Genesis 1:28. It is then repeated to Noah after the flood in Genesis 9:1. Can you explain the "dominion mandate?" Does it apply today?

5. How does Psalm 8 amplify the Christian's understanding of the dominion mandate? What are the implications of Psalm 8 for the radical environmentalists' claims that it is presumptuous and wrong for man to act as if he has greater worth than other "less evolved" species of animals?

6. "Environmental determinism" teaches that the environment determines the potential of man and human civilization. What do you suppose environmental determinists believe about claims that advanced civilizations once lived comfortably in the Amazon jungle?

7. "Environmental pantheism" is both a political agenda and a religious faith. It is a belief system that teaches that because nature is a god and "god" is in nature, therefore the perceived priorities of the planet supersede the priorities of man. Consequently, governments should enforce laws that protect the planet against men exercising the dominion mandate. Explain how Romans 1 and 2 address in part the problem of environmental pantheism and reveal it as a religious faith.

8. From a spiritual perspective, are there any fundamental differences between Amazonian tribesmen who worship the earth goddess, and modern environmentalists who see the earth as the life force for humanity?

9. What is a "carbon footprint," and why are environmentalists so concerned about it?

10. If many of the varieties of giant trees in the Amazon can replenish themselves and grow to enormous heights in less than the life span of a human, then what are the implications of this growth rate for logging and deforestation in the Amazon?

## Episode 2

# The Mystery of the Lost Legacy of Adventure and Evangelism

For 500 years, explorers have gone to the Amazon. They have braved death by poison darts, malaria, and starvation, all in the hope of discovery. Some searched for El Dorado, others sought to be the first to chronicle strange creatures. Many of these explorers never returned, and their stories remain shrouded in mystery even as their legacies have been largely swallowed by the forest itself.

But there is an even better reason to go to the Amazon rainforest—a holy reason, one born out of an ancient mandate to subdue the earth: it is the call of dominion. Those who accept this call must hunger for discovery. They must take upon themselves the mantle of naturalist, explorer, and husbandman of creation, and they must do so for the one true King of the Amazon rainforest: Jesus Christ.

Watch "The Mystery of the Lost Legacy of Adventure and Dominion," and then answer the following study questions to document what you learned.

# Study Questions

## Part 1

1. What are some of the lessons we can learn from the many reasons Teddy Roosevelt desired to explore the Amazon?

2. What biblical principles are evident in Kermit's response to the physical needs and challenges faced by his father, Teddy Roosevelt, during their exploration in the Amazon? What Scripture passages can we draw from to help us think through helping others in need, preservation of life, and commitment to our fathers?

3. What role does dominion play in the Great Commission? As we disciple the nations and steward the creation God has given us, how does this affect culture and civilization around us?

4. Is the Amazon inherently inhospitable? Is there evidence that civilizations have survived or possibly even thrived in the Amazon in the past? If so, who and when?

5. How do the native people find their way through the jungle without paths?

6. What are some biblical passages and principles that help shape a Christian perspective on doing hard things, exploration, and even things that may be a bit fearful and stretch us?

7. What do the Scriptures say about the creation praising the Creator? How should this influence our attitude and disposition toward the Creator of the universe (Psalm 69:24, 96:11-12, 98:7-8; Isaiah 44:23, 49:13, 55:12-13)?

8. What does recounting God's providences of the past, and "story-telling," have to do with stewardship and dominion? Why is it important to record and relate our experiences (Exodus 13:14; Deuteronomy 4:32, 32:7; Job 8:8-10; Psalm 44:1, 77:5, 78:3-4, 143:5)?

9. How does biblical stewardship differ from environmental pantheism and industrialism?

## Part 2

1. What is the origin of the name "Amazon"?

2. Give some definition to the size of the Amazon in breadth and width. How does this compare to the size of United States?

3. Who was Percy Fawcett, and what is his significance to the Amazon?

4. What is the significance of 1542 in the history of the Amazon?

5. What is the City of Z, also known as El Dorado? What was its fascination to Percy Fawcett and other Europeans?

6. What are some of the perils of the Amazon documented by Percy Fawcett? What are some of the ways explorers and missionaries of the past died in the rainforest?

7. How have documented explorations into the Amazon, both in the past and present, challenged many common notions about the primitive nature of the peoples of the region and their development of civilization in the forest?

8. What is the role of man in the Amazon in light of Psalm 8 and Matthew 28:18-20?

9. What is environmental determinism, and how is it contrary to what the Bible teaches?

10. What does the Bible say about worshipping the creation instead of the Creator (Romans 1:18-32)?

11. What are some of the objects God references in the book of Job to establish his authority in the face of his creature (Job) questioning Him (Job 38-41)? What lessons can we learn from similar observations?

# For Further Reference

**Warning:** The resources listed below were selected because they contain helpful research, commentary, or stories which can add greatly to your study of the mysteries of the Amazon, but please be aware that Vision Forum Ministries may not endorse certain aspects or themes in some of these works.

*The River of Doubt: Theodore Roosevelt's Darkest Journey,* by Candice Millard

**Please Note:** *The River of Doubt: Theodore Roosevelt's Darkest Journey* contains a false understanding of Evolutionary theory. Readers must critically evaluate comments in light of Scripture. We are recommending this resource because it is the best source on Roosevelt's expedition into the Amazon.

*The Lost City of Z: A Tale of Deadly Obsession in the Amazon*, by David Grann

**Please Note:** *The Lost City of Z: A Tale of Deadly Obsession in the Amazon* contains very intense and graphic descriptions of team members' interactions with insects, animals, and infection.

*Tools of Dominion: The Case Laws of Exodus,* by Gary North

"God's Dominion Mandate and the Nations Today," by Henry Morris, Ph.D.
www.icr.org/article/gods-dominion-mandate-nations-today/

"Dominion Mandate," by Henry Morris, Ph.D.
www.icr.org/article/dominion-mandate/

"Adam and the Animals," by Henry Morris, Ph.D.
www.icr.org/article/339/

*Mysteries of the Ancient World: A Christian Interpretation of Great Controversies of Earth History,* by Douglas W. Phillips

# Episode 3
# The Mystery of the Strange Creatures of the Amazon

There is a relentless beauty to the animal kingdom of the Amazon. From the majestic macaws soaring overhead to the bright pink dolphins of the jungle tributaries, this is a world teeming with life—brilliant life, colorful life, life that is found nowhere else on planet Earth. Some of these colors can almost be heard.

It is a world in which ants sing in the morning, bats yelp in the black of night, and sloths whine under the noon-day sun. But it's no Eden, and it's no world for the faint of heart. From the microscopic to the gargantuan, there are thousands of human-threatening species of organisms, insects, fish, and reptiles. But despite the pervasive dangers of this lost world, the creatures of the Amazon beckon us with stories, and each creature has one—a story that speaks to their splendor, to their complexity, and above all, to the wisdom of their Creator.

Yet questions persist. Who are these strange creatures? Why do some thrive in this world and in no other? What about the legends of even more mysterious creatures, creatures known to the people of the Amazon but as yet undocumented by modern science? And, most of all, what is their message? The answer to this last question is not elusive. It is available to all who have eyes to see and ears to hear. Because if you stop, look, and listen very carefully, amidst the glorious colors and movements of this exotic biosphere of life you will hear a symphony of praise played on living instruments by the orchestra of the mysterious in the greatest concert hall on Earth: the Amazon rainforest.

Watch "The Mystery of the Strange Creatures of the Amazon," and then answer the following study questions to document what you learned.

# Study Questions

1. Can you find a Scripture passage that speaks to a God-given separation between man and the animal kingdom?

2. Evolutionists describe man as an animal. The Bible makes it clear that man was created distinct in nature, purpose, and identity from the animal kingdom. What is the most important and fundamental difference between the creation of man and the creation of animals?

3. God created each kind of animal with a specific purpose for this earth. With the introduction of death at the time of the Fall of Man, animals changed in several distinct ways. What are some of those ways?

4. The Bible indicates that even in a fallen world the wisdom of the design and interaction of life within the animal kingdom is not only a reflection of the mercy and loving kindness of God for man on this earth, it is also an evidence of the wisdom and glory of the Creator. Can you defend this principle from Scripture?

5. The changing water levels of the Amazon rainforest make it a difficult environment for most mammals. With this in mind, why do you believe that mammals such as monkeys and sloths thrive in the rainforest? What about tapirs and capybaras?

6. What evidence is there from Scripture that the animals of the Amazon rainforest actually communicate praise to the Lord?

7. When men begin to exercise dominion over the earth by bringing it into subjection, animals that tend to be dangerous to man begin to disappear. Why?

8. Is there a special biblical enmity that exists between men and serpents based on Genesis 3:15 or other passages? If so, does this factor into the terror that creatures like the anaconda often inspire in others? Does it surprise you to know that most of the ancient pagan tribes of the Amazon and Peru believed that the serpent was the true god to be worshipped and that it brought knowledge to the people from the underworld?

9. Many of the Amazon natives' beliefs about the legendary "yacumama" may seem hard for to modern men to believe. On the other hand, there appears to be ample, historical, credible evidence that gigantic snakes have existed in the past and may continue to exist in the Amazon. Can you think of a fire-breathing, plated, water creature described in the Bible that many secularists have dismissed as legend but that the Bible presents as absolute fact?

10. Tarantulas are one of the heartiest creatures of the Amazon. They are remarkably fast, can thrive in trees and in the brush, and survive on a diet of insects and small creatures. What do you suppose their primary contribution is to the ecosystem of the rainforest?

11. The *Into the Amazon* team met many Peruvians who had strong opinions about eating monkeys. Some viewed monkey flesh as a delicacy. Others thought it was improper to eat primates because of their allegedly close relationship to homo-sapiens. Do you believe it is proper to eat monkey meat? Why or why not? Can you make your case from Scripture?

12. Defend from Scripture the following statement: God requires men to deal compassionately and justly with the animal kingdom.

______________________________________________________________________

______________________________________________________________________

______________________________________________________________________

______________________________________________________________________

# Episode 4
# The Mystery of the Plants of the Amazon

We live in a world of pills. Billions of them are produced each year for Americans by our pharmaceutical industry. Do you have a cold? There's a pill for that. Do you feel depressed? There's a pill for that. Are your children misbehaving? Yes, there's even a pill for that. There seems to be a pill for just about everything.

But in an age when our food sources are being reengineered and genetically manipulated in laboratories, and when the pharmaceuticals of modern medicine are too often the result of corporate priorities and political outcomes, many are beginning to wonder if somewhere along the way we've gotten off track about the issue of health. Have we perhaps forgotten some of the basics?

This is why so many are now looking to a world that had long been forgotten. From environmentalists to corporate America to government agencies engaged in medical research, the Amazon rainforest is getting new attention.

Some have described the Amazon as the lungs of our planet. Thanks to its rich, vast biodiversity, the continuous recycling of carbon dioxide by the Amazon plant kingdom produces twenty percent of the world's fresh oxygen.

But the Amazon is also a living medical cabinet, one containing thousands of species of flora, at least some of which have providentially corrective properties beneficial to the health of man. And with two-thirds of the world's plants species found in the Amazon, there's a new question on the table: Could it be that the greatest treasure yet to be found from this lost world is in the chemical composition of its plant kingdom?

One of the great problems with a false religious worldview of environmentalism is its tendency to glorify all things tribal. So we shouldn't be surprised that a religious worldview that views man as a plague of carbon footprints would also consider advanced technology, civilization, and even medical research as problematic. On the other hand, our often politicized medical research machine has, until recently, basically ignored much of the information accumulated over generations of research and study by people living in the Amazon about the helpful properties of its plants.

So what is the significance of the plants of the Amazon for us today?

Watch "The Mystery of the Plants of the Amazon," and then answer the following study questions to document what you learned.

# Study Questions

1. What is biodiversity?

______________________________________________

______________________________________________

______________________________________________

2. How does carbon dioxide help create fresh oxygen? What is that process called? Why is the Amazon region so significant to this process?

______________________________________________

______________________________________________

______________________________________________

______________________________________________

______________________________________________

______________________________________________

3. What tree brought Western industrialization and Charles Goodyear to South America? How did Goodyear's discovery help and hurt the indigenous people of the Amazon?

4. What is peculiar about the growth process in the Amazon? What does this mean for archeology, for reforestation?

5. As Christians committed to biblical dominion, we should desire to learn everything we can about God's creation and how natural properties throughout creation can be used for our good. Name several plants and herbs found in the Amazon that might be used to assist in medical treatments.

6. American pharmaceutical companies have largely moved away from natural resources and now use synthetic, manmade medicines as an alternative. Explain potential benefits and drawbacks of this practice. Consider the admonition by Paul to Timothy in 1 Timothy 5:23. How should this influence our perspective on healing agents for medicinal health purposes?

7. Explain the difference and distinctions between:

   A. Elevating all things tribal and embracing mind-altering rituals, superstition, scarification, and consumption of biblically prohibited elements such as blood

   B. Exercising godly stewardship and dominion activity in utilizing natural elements throughout creation

8. How should Psalm 104 influence our perspective on the Amazon rainforest?

# Episode 5
# The Mystery of the Lost Tribes

On May 25, 2007, they appeared for the first time. Many of their bodies were painted red, and some black. In their arms they wielded spears and blow-dart guns, and they pointed at the low-flying bush plane.

In 1988, another previously unknown tribe appeared. Nearly twenty years later, eighty delegates of the Nukak-Makú tribe emerged from the Colombian Amazon to join the modern world. They had several burning questions, including "Do the planes overhead fly on invisible roads?"

The Amazon is so thick, so expansive, and so difficult to negotiate that even in the second decade of the twenty-first century there are still at least 60 tribes who have never made contact with, or who live in isolation from, modern civilization. Their world remains extremely dangerous to outsiders. As recently as the middle of the twentieth century, evangelical Christian missionaries were still being martyred by tribes of headhunters and cannibals. And since the 1970s, hundreds of workers who came into proximity of these tribes have been killed.

More than 43% of the Peruvian people are estimated to come from indigenous tribes. Some are members of a community in transition, while many are fully integrated into modern society. But while scarification and tattooing is on the rise in Western culture, the children of the once-painted tribes of the Amazon are increasingly shunning the paganism of their parents, exchanging face-markings for facials and bare feet for sneakers. Today they are bank tellers, taxi drivers, and pastors, but fifty years ago their grandfathers were cannibals.

The Amazon is a world of dramatic cultural transitions, and one of the rare locations on the planet where truck drivers, fishermen, and ferocious isolated tribes all live within fifty miles of each other. Yet despite all these changes, many questions about this world remain shrouded in mystery.

Biblical chronologists have clues from Scripture about the origin of many of the great nations of the world, from Egypt to China to the peoples of Africa and Europe. But what of the South Americans? Where did they come from? How did they get to South America? When did they arrive?

One thing seems clear: the Amazon is at the end of an era, an epic of time that is disappearing before our eyes and will be gone during our grandchildren's generation. Are these transitions for the best? That of course depends, because the answer rests on our understanding of the nature and meaning of civilization, and the hopeful impact of Christianity on the culture of the mysterious world of the Amazon.

Watch "The Mystery of the Lost Tribes," and then answer the following study questions to document what you learned.

# Study Questions

1. Is there reason to believe that there are still unknown and undiscovered tribes within the Amazon rainforest? Why? What does this say about what is left to be discovered in the Amazon?

2. Are tribes in the Amazon still hostile towards visitors? When was the last recorded aggressive attack against visitors?

3. Why are the terms “original people” and “first people” not accurate to use for the tribal people of the Amazon?

4. What does “indigenous” mean, and why is that term a more accurate description of the Amazon's tribal people?

5. What is the myth of "primitive man"? How does the Bible refute this?

6. What is the myth of the "noble savage"? How does the Bible refute this?

7. Biblical Christianity is attacked and targeted by evolutionists and environmental pantheists because of the necessary implications of a Christian worldview—the necessary implications of the gospel message. What are some of these implications?

8. The Great Commission involves more than presenting the gospel message of salvation. The Great Commission involves bringing cultures to greater maturity and conformity to the ways of Jesus Christ, "teaching them to observe all things that I have commanded you." What does that look like practically? Consider Matthew 28:18-20.

# Episode 6
# The Mystery of the Ica Stones and the Great Peruvian Desert

The greatest mystery of South America is also the most shocking. Buried under sand and sealed within ancient vaults, revealed on lines and glyphs stretched across the Nazca plains, and etched on thousands of stones removed from pre-Colombian archaeological deposits are the clues to a very strange lost world.

In this world, and long before Galileo, men used advanced optics to chart the stars and the comets. Their physicians employed technologies which exceeded those available to Western scientists of the nineteenth century as they performed successful surgeries on the heart and the brain.

If this record is true, if the countless evidences found on desert lines and preserved in works of pottery and stone are accurate, then it was also a world in which man domesticated, fought, and even rode on monsters—monsters that look identical to dinosaurs.

Evolutionists assure us that the ancient people of Peru could not have known such creatures. How could they know of animals that died out millions of years ago and which were not even discovered in the fossil record until the nineteenth century? Herein lies the problem.

At the heart of the mystery of the great Peruvian desert, the Nazca lines, and the Ica stones is a point of antithesis between competing faiths—a controversy that dares to shatter worldviews, and one which uses the artifacts of the pagan deities of the past to expose the nakedness of the humanistic gods of the present before the faithful testimonies of the one true God of eternity.

Watch "The Mystery of the Ica Stones and the Great Peruvian Desert," and then answer the following study questions to document what you learned.

# Study Questions

1. If the Ica stones are authentic and hundreds of years old, how do the medical procedures displayed on the stones refute the evolutionary concept of primitive man?

2. If the Ica stones are authentic and only hundreds of years old, not thousands of years old, how do the images of dinosaur-like creatures being subdued by men refute the evolutionary model? Give a Biblical apologetic/defense of dinosaurs and man dwelling together (Genesis 1:24-31; Job 40:-41:10).

3. What alternate explanation can you offer to those who suggest that the Nazca lines must have been formed by aliens?

4. If we assume that the Nazca lines were drawn by terrestrial man, what does that say about the indigenous people of hundreds of years ago and their understanding of mathematics and geometry? How does this affect the claims of an evolutionary model's description of primitive man?

5. What are some of the fossils that have been found in the Peruvian desert?

6. How do fossils in the Peruvian desert offer supplemental evidence in support of a world-wide Noahic flood? Research and document other "odd" locations where fossils have been found throughout the world, such as mountains (Genesis 6).

# For Further Reference

**Warning:** The resources listed below were selected because they contain helpful research, commentary, or stories which can add greatly to your study of the mysteries of the Amazon, but please be aware that Vision Forum Ministries may not endorse certain aspects or themes in some of these works.

*The Genesis Record*, by Henry Morris, Ph.D

*The Genesis Flood*, by John Whitcomb, Ph.D, and Henry Morris, Ph.D

*The Puzzle of Ancient Man*, by Donald Chittick

*The Mystery in Acambaro*, by Charles H. Hapgood

*Chariots of the Gods,* by Erich von Daniken
(The classic false perspective on the alien hypothesis.)

## Episode 7

# The Mystery of Machu Picchu and the Mighty Inca Empire

Hidden within the haunting vistas of the world's largest mountain range are the remains of a lost kingdom that once dominated a continent. For nearly half a millennium the empire of the mighty Incas ruled South America, and they developed a culture and a religious worldview that continues to influence millions long after its demise.

The crown jewel of this civilization was a mountaintop fortress named Machu Picchu. Looming thousands of feet above the Urubamba river, and hidden within the impenetrable peaks of the Andes Mountains, it was an elite civilization wrought in stone, where the life and luxuries of the leaders of this lost world were on display. It was a world of builders—stonemasons who mastered the art of carving, quarrying, and laying massive stones with such precision that they had no rival in the ancient world.

But Machu Picchu was also a place of blood, where pagan priests offered human sacrifices to the sky, the mountain, and the snake god of the underworld.

In 1492, at the height of its power, the world of the Incas covered 380,000 miles. It stretched from Ecuador to Chile, and encompassed portions of Bolivia, Peru, Argentina, and Colombia. But in less than 50 years the Incan empire would disappear. When it died, many of the Incas' secrets were lost as well, waiting for the day that the stories of the secret chambers, buried mummies, and pagan altars would be revealed to the modern world. For Machu Picchu, that day has come. And with the discovery of this once great high place of paganism, the world has been presented with a visible testimony in stone of what happens to cultures that worship creation rather than the Creator.

Watch "The Mystery of Machu Picchu and the Mighty Inca Empire," and then answer the following study questions to document what you learned.

## Study Questions

1. How are environmental pantheists and revisionist historians rewriting the story of the legacy and conquest of the Incas, and why is this revisionism important to their social and political agenda?

2. What are some of the unique elements of the Incan architectural system?

3. For centuries, the Incas were a seemingly invincible force. Then in the span of mere months they were destroyed by a force less than 1/1000th of their strength. How did this happen, and why?

4. The story is as old as Cain and Abel: brother vs. brother battles that change the world. How did sibling rivalry contribute to the destruction of the Inca empire?

5. Were the Spanish conquistadors righteous agents of change against the Incas, wicked usurpers, or something else?

6. What happens to the religious faith and infrastructure of a nation when leaders who claim to be gods are proven to be men? Consider what happened to Japan in World War II. How does this relate to the story of the Incas?

7. At a time when the descendants of pagan tribesmen are seeking to break with the badges of idolatry like scarification, tattoos, and body mutilation, American Christians are turning back to the symbols of ancient pagan idolatry. Why? What should we do about this?

8. What is the generational legacy of Hiram Bingham? What do the life missions of his grandfather, father, himself, and his son say about the impact of a father's vision on the vision of a son?

9. What was Hiram Bingham's motivation to search for Machu Picchu? What facilitated him finding the ancient city after it had been lost for so many hundreds of years?

10. What was the significance of Machu Picchu to the Incan Empire? Who lived there, and what was their economy?

# Study Guide Answer Key

# Episode 1
# The Mystery of the Meaning of the Amazon

## Question 1

### A. Importance of Taxonomy

1. **Genesis 2:19** – God brought every animal to Adam for him to name. This was important because, from the very beginning, God was establishing that man was to identify, evaluate, and classify the animals for the glory of the Creator.

2. **Genesis 7:2-3** – The Lord commanded that Noah take seven of every clean animal, male and female; and two of each animal that was unclean, male and female ; and seven of each of the birds of the air, male and female. In this case, God was calling Noah to the task of taxonomy for preservation of the created kinds to survive into the post-flood world.

3. **Book of Job** – After Job cried out to God for an answer, the Lord answered Job by pointing out some of His most amazing animals to establish Himself

as the Creator, worthy to be praised for His great creation.

4. **Animals of the Bible** – The Bible mentions hundreds of animals. Many times the Lord uses the attributes of these animals to teach the characteristics of man and/or the traits of Himself, or object lessons from the attributes of certain animals. Another example is when the law was given, and man was commanded to classify animals as clean and unclean.

B. Stewardship of Gardens

1. **Genesis 2:15** – God placed Adam in the garden and told him to tend it. He also commanded him not to eat from the Tree of the Knowledge of Good and Evil (verse 17). This is when the first battle took place: how do we use the natural environment around us? Adam chose to use it improperly. He used it for his own glory. So we shouldn't be surprised when, to this very day, we see the same sorts of battles over the allocation of resources. Men have always been engaged in a huge battle over the issue of the environment and the issue of dominion.

C. Trees and Spiritual Lessons

1. **Genesis 2:17** – One of the lessons from the Tree of the Knowledge of Good and Evil was establishing how creation was to be used. Would it be in harmony with the Lord's command, or with man's disobedience?

2. **Mark 11:12-24** – Jesus cursed the fig tree because it bore no fruit.

3. **Revelation 22: 2** – The Tree of Life will be found in the New Jerusalem.

4. **Trees of the Bible** – There are more than thirty different trees mentioned in the Bible. Many times trees represent nations, or people, or are used as symbols to teach spiritual lessons.

# Question 2

A. The Amazon rainforest is under the curse of sin. The Garden of Eden, prior to the fall, was not.

B. The Amazon rainforest can be a dangerous place, with thorns, thistles, and deadly animals. The Garden of Eden, prior to the fall, bore no danger.

C. The Amazon rainforest is the site of the death and decay of animals, people, and plants. The Garden of Eden, prior to the fall, had no death or decay.

D. The Amazon rainforest is a showcase for predator/prey relationships. The Garden of Eden, prior to the fall, contained no predators.

E. The Amazon rainforest is filled with death, pain, and suffering. The Garden of Eden, prior to the fall, had no suffering.

F. The Amazon rainforest, with a post-flood environment, is imperfect. Although it contains many varieties of plants, it also lacks many other plants and animals, making it different from the Garden of Eden environment.

## Question 3

A. The Amazon rainforest covers over 1.4 billion acres.

B. One-fifth of the world's fresh water flows through the Amazon—six million cubic feet of water dumps into the Atlantic Ocean every second.

C. Estimates indicate that there are 400 trees per acre in the Amazon Rain Forest.

## Question 4

A. The Dominion Mandate (originally given in Genesis 1:26 and repeated several times throughout the Scriptures) was God's directive to man to classify and steward creation for God's glory and man's benefit. The duty of man under the direction and guidance of God, according to His will, as directed by His Word, is to steward all of creation and all that we do according to His pleasure. This important doctrine, the doctrine of dominion, is unavoidable—all mankind exercises dominion. The question is, for whom are we exercising dominion? Are we exercising dominion for our own glory? For humanistic and vain efforts? Or, are we exercising dominion and stewardship of our efforts and this world for the glory of the Creator of the entire universe, God Himself? The dominion mandate still applies today (Psalm 8:6).

# Question 5

A. Psalm 8 amplifies the Christian's understanding of the dominion mandate by defining man in the proper context of creation. The Lord God is worthy of praise because of His creation. The Creator is the omnipotent One. Compared to the Creator, man is lowly. But, He is lofty compared to the rest of God's creation, being made a little lower than the angels. And, the Creator has entrusted him to have dominion over all things He has created.

B. The implications for radical environmentalists are huge. Because He is the Creator, God establishes the worth of all things. In Psalm 8, the Lord clearly communicates the order given in creation: man has been crowned with glory and honor, and all things have been put under his feet. This is clearly distinct from, and the opposite of, environmentalism which seeks to devalue human life and to give animals and the earth itself equal value to humans.

# Question 6

A. Many believe that men and women are bound by their environments, and that ultimately they are a product of their environments. Furthermore, evolutionary theory suggests mankind started out simple, and has slowly increased in intelligence and sophistication. For this reason, many would believe that people living in the jungle would necessarily be primitive and backward. However, a biblical worldview teaches that man was intelligent from the very beginning. And, because of the dominion mandate, he is able to rise above environmental influences and steward his natural surroundings by taming the wild and bringing it into submission for his benefit.

# Question 7

A. Romans 1 states that unregenerate men suppress the truth in unrighteousness. It says their hearts are darkened, and though they profess to be wise they become fools. Furthermore, they exchange the truth for a lie and worship the creation instead of the Creator. Romans 1 makes it clear that all are without excuse for this sin, since all clearly deny the evidence of God which is around them and which bears witness in their conscience.

# Question 8

A. The tribes of the ancient earth and the modern world are separated by centuries, but not by substance. Modern Western culture has Hollywood, which makes movies communicating a message that we must preserve the sanctity of nature. Modern Western culture is indoctrinated by legislation from civil government through adopted laws which elevate the protection of animals above the unborn. Our modern Western culture politicians, even the UN, discuss the possibility of giving the earth human rights! Sadly, modern environmentalists worship nature just like Amazonian tribesmen—and this is true of all fallen cultures throughout the world and history.

# Question 9

A. A carbon footprint refers to the chemical element carbon and the greenhouse gas emissions that our actions produce. This measurement is important to those who believe greenhouse gasses are the cause of climate change. Recently, the phrase "reduce your carbon footprint" has become a way to say that we all need to cut down on our personal impact on the planet. If evolution was true, and nature is all that there is, then mankind must be responsible for saving the planet. However, although we must responsibly steward all resources and exercise care for that which God has given us, it is God alone who upholds all things (Colossians 1:17). Heaven and Earth will not pass away until such a time as He has ordained.

# Question 10

A. The rapidity of tree growth in the Amazon rainforest provides excellent opportunity for man, using wisdom in his stewardship and careful planning, to utilize that resource more frequently than in other environments where similar growth may take two or three or ten times as long. This utilization can be done in the Amazon without destroying the broader rainforest.

Episode 2

# The Mystery of the Lost Legacy of Adventure and Evangelism

**Part 1**

## Question 1

Among the many lessons we can learn from Teddy Roosevelt's explorations in the Amazon, following are three significant observations:

A. A sense of adventure and exploration as we investigate creation to better utilize and steward the resources God has given us.

B. Seizing opportunity to disciple our children by mentoring them in each of our practical explorations.

C. Vigilance in the midst of hardship, challenge and opposition.

# Question 2

A. Kermit was willing to personally sacrifice to preserve his father's life.

B. Scriptures

1. Helping Others in Need

   a. **John 15:13** – "Greater love has no one than this, than to lay down one's life for his friends."

   b. **Luke 10:30-37** – Parable of the Good Samaritan.

   c. **1 John 3:16** – "By this we know love, because He laid down His life for us. And we also ought to lay down *our* lives for the brethren."

2. Preservation of Life

   a. **Psalm 82:3** – "Defend the poor and fatherless; Do justice to the afflicted and needy."

   b. **Job 34:28** – "So that they cause the cry of the poor to come unto him, and he heareth the cry of the afflicted."

   c. **Proverbs 31:9** – "Open thy mouth, judge righteously, and plead the cause of the poor and needy."

3. Commitment to Our Fathers

   a. **Ephesians 6:1-3** – "Children, obey your parents in the Lord, for this is right. *Honor your father and mother*, which is the first commandment with promise: "*that it may be well with you and you may live long on the earth*."

   b. **Deuteronomy 32:7** – "Remember the days of old, Consider the years of many generations. Ask your father, and he will show you; Your elders, and they will tell you."

# Question 3

A. To fulfill the command of the Great Commission our duty is to teach the nations all things whatsoever Jesus Christ has commanded us. This duty includes communicating obedience to all of the commands and prohibitions of Scripture, including our duty to steward and exercise dominion for the Creator's glory. If we neglect to teach all of the counsel of God, then we neglect to exercise obedience and dominion in proclaiming the true gospel of Jesus Christ. To exclude all or any of the commands of Jesus Christ from our disciple-making process is to alter the gospel from what God commanded into a man-devised message which is incomplete, shows lack of obedience, lack of stewardship, and an exercise of dominion that is not yielded to the instruction of God Himself.

B. The true gospel message transforms every aspect of life. We are to take all of our thoughts captive to the obedience of Jesus Christ (2 Corinthians 10:5). As we are transformed by the renewing of our minds (Romans 12:2), this leads to obedience to Christ and better standards of life and better stewardship as we display the acceptable, and perfect, will of God.

# Question 4

A. All essential elements for survival are present in the Amazon: air, water, and food. While the Amazon does provide many challenges, man can overcome those dangers as he takes dominion over the natural environment.

B. Early Spanish explorers learned about the accounts of lost civilizations in the Amazon. In the 1500s, Spaniards like Francisco de Orellana led expeditions to find these great cities. In 1925, a British explorer named Percival Fawcett also led an expedition to find a great city of gold. In modern times, large cities of the Amazon had been thought to be only legends. However, in 2010 a team of researchers found exciting new evidence of huge civilizations that once lived in the rainforest.

# Question 5

A. One of the techniques displayed during this episode of *Into the Amazon* including marking the shrubs and plants along the trail with machete hatch marks. Approximately every ten feet, a mark is cut into the side of a tree. To return, one simply follows the marks.

# Question 6

A. **Isaiah 41:10** – "Fear not, for I *am* with you; Be not dismayed, for I *am* your God. I will strengthen you, Yes, I will help you, I will uphold you with My righteous right hand."

B. **Psalm 34:7-9** – "The angel of the LORD encamps all around those who fear Him, And delivers them. Oh, taste and see that the LORD *is* good; Blessed *is* the man *who* trusts in Him! Oh, fear the LORD, you His saints! *There is* no want to those who fear Him."

C. **Psalm 46:1** – "God *is* our refuge and strength, A very present help in trouble."

D. **Philippians 4:6-7** – "Be anxious for nothing, but in everything by prayer and supplication, with thanksgiving, let your requests be made known to God; and the peace of God, which surpasses all understanding, will guard your hearts and minds through Christ Jesus."

E. **2 Timothy 1:7** – "For God has not given us a spirit of fear, but of power and of love and of a sound mind."

# Question 7

A. Each of the passages listed with this question teach us that all of creation praises the Creator. Like Romans 1 states, God's attributes may be seen through the things He has made. All of this world and all of creation is a testimony to His greatness.

B. All of creation should worship the Creator. As the stewards over His creation, we should acknowledge His greatness and worship with joy and gratitude for His goodness and mercy. Furthermore, His creation should provoke humility and wonder as we consider the great position of privilege which God has extended to us, being made a little lower than the angels.

# Question 8

A. By learning and recounting stories of the past, we learn to better understand God's sovereign hand through all of history. By remembering the past we should be provoked to gratitude, encouraged in God's covenantal faithfulness, and stirred toward greater obedience.

> *"The march of Providence is so slow and our desires so impatient; the work of progress so immense and our means of aiding it so feeble; the life of humanity is so long, that of the individual so brief, that we often see only the ebb of the advancing wave and are thus discouraged. It is history that teaches us to hope."*
> —Robert E. Lee

B. God commands us to "remember the days of old" so that we will not forget His faithfulness in the past.

# Question 9

A. Biblical stewardship recognizes the dominion mandate that has been given by the Creator Himself, and all things are subject to His will and pleasure. Our stewardship must reflect God's priorities to bring Him glory.

B. Environmental pantheism teaches that the earth is the "mother" of all created life, and that "preservation" of natural resources is of supreme importance and priority even over the preservation of man. Environmental pantheism devalues human life and worships nature.

C. Industrialism prioritizes personal utilitarian gain through exploitation of resources without regard for responsible stewardship and preservation.

**Part 2**

# Question 1

A. Francisco de Orellanas described a group of warrior women in the rainforest as Amazonians, after the fabled stories from Rome. Eventually the basin and river took on the name Amazonus after the legendary warrior women these conquistadors saw.

# Question 2

A. The Amazon River Basin is about 4,195 miles long and about 648 miles wide.

B. The Amazon encompasses one-fifth the size of the continental United States.

# Question 3

A. Percy Fawcett was a British explorer who in 1925 led a team in hope of locating a great city of gold, which he called The City of Z. While Fawcett exemplified the spirit of adventure and exploration, he and his team disappeared in the Amazon, and were never seen again. Like other explorers looking for a city of gold, Fawcett was considered to be looking for nothing more than a legendary place. Recent discoveries and evidence point to great civilizations of the past thriving in the Amazon region, which could vindicate the pursuits of many explorers. Fawcett's exploration provided data which has been helpful as we explore great cities that once existed in the Amazon, and which aids us in our search today.

# Question 4

A. In 1542, Francisco de Orellanas began an exploration with a group of conquistadors that broke off from a larger group of thousands who were searching for the fabled city of El Dorado. The earliest conquistadors, like Orellanas, came to South America and spoke with local tribes where they learned of a mighty civilization, one adorned with gold, that existed deep, deep in the Amazon rainforest.

# Question 5

A. Fawcett and the Europeans had heard accounts concerning large cities filled with gold. Their goal was to find and explore these cities.

# Question 6

A. Fawcett described the Amazon like this: "A poisoned hell that could never be explored on foot, 60 foot anacondas capable of picking a man out of a canoe, savage ape men, an infested plain of deadly snakes, bats so big they looked like pterodactyls, ferocious black panthers, white Indian tribes, swarms of biting bees, fires in the distance."

B. There are several ways to die in the jungle. You can be attacked by insects like the bot fly and become sick with malaria, or yellow fever. Another option is to be attacked by venomous snakes, or by the anaconda that will crush you to death. A common way to die is through starvation. And a fourth way may include your body being filled with poison darts and arrows launched by local tribes people. However, the death of choice is probably slipping and falling down a mountainside or a cliff.

# Question 7

A. Explorers of the past assumed the tribal peoples of the Amazon region were simplistic and "primitive". Modern evidence of vast cities and complex infrastructure turns the notion of unlearned culture upside down. Recent discoveries reveal advanced waterways, intricate tracking of the sun, moon, and seasons, and architecture constructed with precision calculations. These thoughtful designs contradict the notion of a society of cave-man-like simpletons.

# Question 8

A. The role of man in the Amazon is no different than the role of man in any other region of the world. Our duty is to take our thoughts captive to the obedience of Jesus Christ and to be transformed by the renewing of our minds. As we ourselves are transformed, we in turn seek to transform our surroundings for the glory of God. In Psalm 8, we find that man has been given authority to steward God's creation. In the Amazon, we are to steward the abundant natural resources for the glory of God. This means being aware of potential threats as well as prudently maximizing the use of each of the resources available. Matthew 28 and the Great Commission make clear that we cannot relegate any portion of the populated world to an area where we do not communicate the gospel and seek to make disciples of Jesus Christ, teaching them all things whatsoever He has taught us. In the Amazon, we want the people to hear the gospel and be transformed, just as we desire to preach the gospel throughout the entire world.

# Question 9

A. Environmental determinism is the belief that man is defined and limited by his environment. However, the Bible teaches that man is defined by his Creator, must conform to the will of his Creator, and has been given authority to steward and govern his environment rather than be governed by it.

# Question 10

A. The Bible clearly teaches that those who worship the creature/creation will turn to vile passions, and that God will give them over to a reprobate mind. Worship of any other object than God Himself is contrary to the first and greatest commandment:

1. **Exodus 20:3** – "Thou shalt have no other gods before me."

2. **Deuteronomy 6:5** – "And thou shalt love the Lord thy God with all thine heart, and with all thy soul, and with all thy might."

3. **Deuteronomy 11:1** – "Therefore thou shalt love the Lord thy God, and keep his charge, and his statutes, and his judgments, and his commandments, alway."

# Question 11

A. In the book of Job, God references animals including the lions, the goat, and what appear to be dinosaurs—the great Leviathan and Behemoth.

B. From these references we can learn the same lesson that Job did as we look at all the animals that God has made. Who made them? Where were we when they were made? Do we truly understand them? Are we able to fully govern them? Our inability to create or even fully govern what has been created should humble us before the One who has created all things. Only God in His magnificent might can create such handiwork. His creation should provoke wonder and inspire worship, not of what has been created, but of the One who created all.

## Episode 3

# The Mystery of the Strange Creatures of the Amazon

## Question 1

A. Scripture Passages

1. **Genesis 1:26** – "Then God said, "Let Us make man in Our image, according to Our likeness; let them have dominion over the fish of the sea, over the birds of the air, and over the cattle, over all the earth and over every creeping thing that creeps on the earth."

2. **Genesis 1:28** – "Then God blessed them, and God said to them, "Be fruitful and multiply; fill the earth and subdue it; have dominion over the fish of the sea, over the birds of the air, and over every living thing that moves on the earth."

3. **Psalm 8:6-9** – "You have made him to have dominion over the works of Your hands; You have put all *things* under his feet, All sheep and oxen — Even

the beasts of the field, The birds of the air, And the fish of the sea That pass through the paths of the seas."

4. **Ecclesiastes 3:21** – "Who knows the spirit of the sons of men, which goes upward, and the spirit of the animal, which goes down to the earth?"

# Question 2

A. Man alone is made in God's image (Gen. 1:26).

B. Man was given dominion over the animals and the rest of creation (Genesis 1:26, 28; Psalm 8).

C. It is by man that sin came into this world, and it is by the God-man Jesus Christ that man may be redeemed from sin (Romans 5:12-15).

# Question 3

A. Animals began to kill each other.

B. Animals began to kill man.

C. Animals adapted attack/defense mechanisms

D. Animals began the predator/prey relationships.

E. Animals live in fear of each other.

F. Animals live in fear of man.

G. Animals, like man, experience death, suffering, and pain.

# Question 4

A. Romans 1 tells us that we can know the attributes of God from the things that are made.

B. In the book of Job, God demonstrates His amazing wisdom and design by giving Job many examples from the animal kingdom (Job 38).

C. Psalm 104 speaks of the wisdom of God, His design of creation, and how it provides for the creatures of the earth.

# Question 5

A. Each of these animals have been given special features and adaptations that allow them to survive in their specialized niche of the Amazon:

1. Monkeys have been specially designed to thrive in the trees of the Amazon.
2. Three-toed sloths are camouflaged when they hang upside down in the trees.
3. Tapirs are made to survive well in the jungle, and are good swimmers.
4. Capybaras have webbed feet for swimming and supporting themselves in the mud.

# Question 6

A. **Psalm 103:22** – "Bless the Lord, all his works in all places of his dominion: bless the Lord, O my soul."

B. **Psalm 145:10** – "All thy works shall praise thee, O Lord; and thy saints shall bless thee."

C. **Psalm 148:7-10** – "Praise the Lord from the earth, ye dragons, and all deeps: Fire, and hail; snow, and vapour; stormy wind fulfilling his word: Mountains, and all hills; fruitful trees, and all cedars: Beasts, and all cattle; creeping things, and flying fowl"

D. **Psalm 150:6** – "Let everything that has breath praise the LORD."

E. **Isaiah 43:20** – "The beast of the field shall honour me, the dragons and the owls: because I give waters in the wilderness, and rivers in the desert, to give drink to my people, my chosen."

# Question 7

A. Through exercising stewardship, man seeks to govern those elements in his surrounding which are harmful.

B. God communicated safety to Israel as part of His covenant blessing for obedience to His word:

1. **Leviticus 26:6** – "And I will give peace in the land, and ye shall lie down, and none shall make you afraid: and I will rid evil beasts out of the land, neither shall the sword go through your land."

2. **Exodus 23:29-30** – "I will not drive them out from before thee in one year; lest the land become desolate, and the beast of the field multiply against thee. By little and little I will drive them out from before thee, until thou be increased, and inherit the land."

3. **2 Kings 17:25** – "And so it was at the beginning of their dwelling there, that they feared not the Lord: therefore the Lord sent lions among them, which slew some of them."

4. **Job 5:23** – "For thou shalt be in league with the stones of the field: and the beasts of the field shall be at peace with thee."

# Question 8

A. In Genesis 3:15, God declared an enmity between the woman and the serpent. Our greatest enmity is with Satan, and because he took upon himself the form of a serpent at the time of the temptation, God declared as part of the judgment and condemnation upon the serpent a particular enmity among the creatures.

B. The fall eliminated the once peaceful relationship between man and all animals, but enmity between man and the serpent was distinguished from all other man-animal interaction. Satan, because of the form he chose in the garden, is now referred to as the "serpent" with a peculiar negative connotation—the serpent itself has become the image to communicate the devil (Revelation 12:9, 12:14, 20:2).

C. Satan has always tried to mimic the true God. His desire is to steal the worship due the Creator. 2 Corinthians 11:13-15 says, "For such *are* false apostles, deceitful workers, transforming themselves into apostles of Christ. And no wonder! For Satan himself transforms himself into an angel of light. Therefore *it is* no great thing if his ministers also transform themselves into ministers of righteousness, whose end will be according to their works."

# Question 9

A. Leviathan (Job 41).

# Question 10

A. Tarantulas are an excellent aid in keeping the insect and rodent populations governed.

# Question 11

A. We know from Genesis 1:26, Genesis 1:28, and Psalm 8 that man is distinct from all animals (evolution is not true), so monkeys are not our close ancestors. Therefore, consuming monkeys is not cannibalism.

B. In Genesis 9:3, God permitted Noah to eat animals as food.

C. Monkeys are not considered "clean", therefore the Israelites were forbidden from eating monkey meat (Leviticus 11; Deuteronomy 14). However, additional passages in the New Testament also must be considered.

1. **Mark 7:18-20** – "And he saith unto them, Are ye so without understanding

also? Do ye not perceive, that whatsoever thing from without entereth into the man, it cannot defile him; Because it entereth not into his heart, but into the belly, and goeth out into the draught, purging all meats? And he said, That which cometh out of the man, that defileth the man."

2. **1 Tim 4:4-5** – "For every creature of God is good, and nothing to be refused, if it be received with thanksgiving: For it is sanctified by the word of God and prayer."

# Question 12

A. **Proverbs 12:10** – "A righteous *man* regards the life of his animal, but the tender mercies of the wicked *are* cruel."

# Episode 4
# The Mystery of the Plants of the Amazon

## Question 1

A. Bio = "involving living organisms." Diversity = "difference." Therefore, biodiversity is the range of differences in a plant or animal. Biodiversity in kinds of plants shows the amazing creativity of our God.

## Question 2

A. Mankind and animals breathe in oxygen and exhale carbon dioxide. Plants take in carbon dioxide, and release oxygen—an amazing balance that points to design.

B. This process is called photosynthesis.

C. Because of the vastness of the Amazon, and the number of plants found throughout the Amazon, it has been estimated that this part of the world produces 20% of the oxygen for the whole world. One-fifth of all of our oxygen is generated from the Amazon rainforest.

# Question 3

A. The rubber tree.

B. The rubber tree improved the economic conditions of the Amazon region through the production of jobs and revenue. Further utilization of natural resources in the Amazon rainforest was an excellent display of stewardship and creativity. However, Western culture's lack of subordination to the will and pleasure of God further influenced the pagans in another form of idolatry through materialism and an unwillingness to confront the lawless customs of many of the tribal peoples: nakedness, fornication, multiple wives, cannibalism, murder, etc. Western culture excused lawless behavior due to insubordination to God, lack of gospel-driven purpose, and an exaltation of environmental determinism and the myth of the "noble savage."

# Question 4

A. Because of optimal conditions including soil, water, and sunlight, plants grow much faster in the Amazon than in other regions of the world.

B. This non-typical growth rate makes it difficult for archeologists to locate sites, and to maintain them once they have been uncovered, due to the maintenance necessary to fight back the plants that threaten to re-cover their dig sites.

C. Reforestation in the Amazon can take place at an incredibly rapid pace. This means that habits for animals, and resources gleaned from the rainforest, are replenished quickly.

# Question 5

A. **Cat Claw** – The bark from this plant can be used to make medicine for treating digestive problems, ulcers, inflammation, and help heal wounds.

B. **Coca** – Used to induce labor.

C. **Chondrodendron tomentosum, better known as curare** – Used as a natural pain suppressor.

D. **Scoparia dulcis, also known as vassourinha** – Grows profusely in the Amazon rainforest and is used to inhibit tumors, reduce blood pressure, reduce pain, and fight viruses.

# Question 6

A. Benefits: Synthetic pharmaceuticals may allow for more broad production and dissemination of critical, health-supplying resources. This may allow for greater economy of scale and lesser expense in its creation. Enhancements of naturally found traits may prove to yield greater results.

B. Disadvantages: As we refine active elements of naturally found properties with medicinal purposes, we may inadvertently alter properties which are helpful if left unaltered. Unknown or unrealized side effects may result from manipulation or abandonment of naturally found properties associated with those elements which contain medicinal value.

C. Paul urged Timothy to care for his body, and acknowledged value in the use of wine for his stomach's sake. This appears to be an indication of medicinal value. (See also Proverbs 31:6. While drunkenness is prohibited, both Paul and the author of Proverbs 31 acknowledge the medicinal value of wine.)

# Question 7

A. 1 Corinthians 6:19-20 says, "What? know ye not that your body is the temple of the Holy Ghost which is in you, which ye have of God, and ye are not your own? For ye are bought with a price: therefore glorify God in your body, and in your spirit, which are God's." Discretion must be applied to distinguish between using what God has given us to optimize our health while taking our thoughts captive to His obedience, and participating in excess through drunkenness or inebriation for pleasure. We must steward both the resource and our bodies which are the temple of the living God (1 Corinthians 3:16-17; Ephesians 5:18).

# Question 8

A. What appears indisputable is the fact that locked within the Amazon rainforest is an entire pharmacy of remedies available to men if only we'll go there and discover, investigate, and then apply what we learn. When we do this, we can better understand the principle of the Psalm 104—God has given every herb to the service of man.

## Episode 5

# The Mystery of the Lost Tribes

## Question 1

A. Yes.

B. Explorers have made contact with several unreached tribes even in recent years. These tribes refer to other tribes within the forest which have not made contact with the rest of civilization.

C. Our lack of knowledge of people groups throughout the Amazon rainforest should humble us and provoke to consider what other significant discoveries we may be ignorant of. The Amazon is thick, vast, and extensive, and we have only begun to uncover evidence of large, remote ancient civilizations.

# Question 2

A. Some tribes that explorers have contacted are very hostile toward visitors. Other tribes are open to visitors.

B. To our knowledge, the last aggressive attack against explorers and outsiders was with bow and arrow, against a helicopter, in May of 2008.

# Question 3

A. "Original people" and "first people" are used to indicate that these tribes originated in the Amazon rainforest region. However, we know from biblical accounts that the dispersion of tribes and confusion of tongues found in Genesis 11 indicate that all peoples emigrated to places around the world, including to Amazonia.

# Question 4

A. The terms "original people" and "first people" communicate the idea that particular people groups have always been in a particular region, whereas the term "indigenous" indicates that a group of people are now living in a particular region. Genesis 11 clearly records the central dispersion of all tongues and tribes from the Tower of Babel.

# Question 5

A. The myth of "primitive man" is the idea that present cultures evolved from more simplistic cultures.

B. Biblical passages show that man was created with intelligence:

   1. Genesis 2:15 illustrates the intelligence of Adam as he was commanded to dress and keep the garden: "And the Lord God took the man, and put him into the garden of Eden to dress it and to keep it." In Genesis 2:19-20, we see

the skill of Adam displayed as he names as classifies all of the animals: "And out of the ground the Lord God formed every beast of the field, and every fowl of the air; and brought them unto Adam to see what he would call them: and whatsoever Adam called every living creature, that was the name thereof. And Adam gave names to all cattle, and to the fowl of the air, and to every beast of the field; but for Adam there was not found an help meet for him."

2. Genesis 4:20-22 says, "And Adah bore Jabal. He was the father of those who dwell in tents and have livestock. His brother's name was Jubal. He was the father of all those who play the harp and flute. And as for Zillah, she also bore Tubal-Cain, an instructor of every craftsman in bronze and iron. And the sister of Tubal-Cain was Naamah." In this passage we see that there were tent-makers, cattle ranchers, musicians, and metal workers very shortly after the creation after Adam and Eve.

3. Genesis 11 recounts the dispersion of the Tower of Babel that took place approximately 1,700 years after creation. As we read this account, we see that, "The people are one and they all have one language, and this is what they begin to do; now nothing that they propose to do will be withheld from them." The unity of the people brought about great skill, skill used for wickedness but nonetheless indicative of advanced civilizations very early in history.

# Question 6

A. The myth of the "noble savage" is the idea that "unevolved man," "uncivilized man," or so-called "primitive man" is morally and culturally superior to technologically advanced civilization and the world of Western civilization.

B. Romans 3:21-26 says that all mankind has fallen into sin and is under the curse of sin (Romans 3:23, 5:15-17). "But now the righteousness of God apart from the law is revealed, being witnessed by the Law and the Prophets, even the righteousness of God, through faith in Jesus Christ, to all and on all who believe. For there is no difference; for all have sinned and fall short of the glory of God, being justified freely by His grace through the redemption that is in Christ Jesus, whom God set forth as a propitiation by His blood, through faith, to demonstrate His righteousness, because in His forbearance God had passed over the sins that were previously committed, to demonstrate at the present time His righteousness, that He might be just and the justifier of the one who has faith in Jesus." The Bible makes it clear that all people are sinful, and that justification and imputation of righteousness may only be imputed through the redemptive sacrifice of Jesus Christ.

# Question 7

A. Christianity requires submission to the One true God and subordination to His will and His pleasure. The greatest commandment is to love the Lord God with all of our heart, all of our soul, and with all of our mind (Mark 12:30). If we love the Lord, we will keep His commandments (John 14:15). We are to be transformed by the renewing of our minds (Romans 12:2), and this will mean transformation of cultures. This imposition upon all of culture is at complete odds with evolutionists and environmental pantheists, as they view the environment as "god." Imposition of God's will and pleasure—His commands—is seen as an intrusion to "natural selection" and "freedom of will," and in this regard their assessment is correct. Antinomianism, evolutionism, and environmental pantheism are at enmity with God.

# Question 8

A. First, we acknowledge that we take dominion under the authority of Christ. Our mission is to make disciples, baptizing and teaching them to observe all of Christ's commands. This means that cultural norms and mores—cultural sins—must be corrected. As we disciple the nations, we teach them to obey all of the ways of God and conform to His will. This includes elimination of fornication, consuming blood, bestiality, stealing, idolatry, murder, and obedience to all of the commands of God.

# Episode 6
# The Mystery of the Ica Stones and the Great Peruvian Desert

## Question 1

A. If the Ica stones are authentic, then images on them displaying medical procedures reveals complex measures being executed by men hundreds of years ago. These records refute the evolutionary notion that "primitive" man must be "simple" and "unevolved." On the contrary, this would be consistent with the biblical account of creation in Genesis 1-2 that reveals Adam's great mental capacity at the beginning of mankind.

# Question 2

A. According to Genesis 1:24-31, both dinosaurs and man were created on the sixth day. All that God created He created in six days (Exodus 20:11). This means dinosaurs as well. Furthermore, in the book of Job (40:1-41:10), God speaks of Behemoth and Leviathan, two creatures that seem to be two dinosaur-like beasts. Job 41:26-29 references how no one can approach this creature with spear, darts, or javelins. With the dinosaur-like descriptions recorded in the Scriptures, and the fact that man, animals, and all that is in this world were created in six days, we have clear biblical evidence of man and dinosaurs dwelling together.

# Question 3

A. An alien hypothesis is rooted in a presupposition that man's intellect was not sufficiently advanced to be able to accomplish such precision drawings without the aid of flight or "aliens." However, we have evidence that early Peruvians tracked the seasons, stars, and sun and moon patterns which clearly reveals their understanding of mathematics. Mariner techniques of solar mapping to aid in direction use similar efforts to chart straight courses and aid in explaining the tremendous precision we see in the Nazca lines.

# Question 4

A. If primitive terrestrial man drew the Nazca lines, then the precision drawing skills necessary to create such mammoth drawings would require an excellent working knowledge of math and geometry to create the drawings over great distances without them becoming skewed.

B. Evidence of elaborate design with mathematical precision betrays idea that ancient men were unintelligent, "unevolved", and simple. And, evidence of complex, intelligent man is contrary to the evolutionary model.

# Question 5

A. Shells.

B. Whales.

C. Sharks.

D. Fish.

E. Turtles.

F. Seals.

G. Porpoises.

H. Ground sloths.

I Penguins.

# Question 6

A. While more research needs to be done in the Peruvian desert, it appears that many aquatic creatures were buried very rapidly and fossilized quickly. This is consistent with the biblical record of a worldwide flood. Deposition of this type and this age is contrary to the evolutionary model, which accounts for vastly different geologic and aquatic conditions millions of years ago, but not merely thousands or a few hundred years ago. Gradual change cannot account for fossilization and preservation on the scale that we find in the Peruvian desert.

B. There are hundreds of sites all around the world in which we see creatures from different environments (sea, land, air) all deposited together in one jumbled mess. There are usually points of commonality at these sites: rapid burial, rapid fossilization, no evidence of decay due to exposure, and association with strong water currents.

## Episode 7

# The Mystery of Machu Picchu and the Mighty Inca Empire

## Question 1

A. Environmental pantheists and revisionist historians record the Incas as simple, unlearned people who were "in tune" with nature. However, Inca ruins clearly display great achievements in technology and civil engineering. Their sanctuaries, tombs, and altars offer evidence documenting that their pagan practices and the worship of nature led to wicked practices such as human sacrifice.

B. Environmental pantheists do not criticize the Incas' worship of nature. Rather they support it, and therefore recount their activities as a noble culture, living in harmony with their environment. Revisionist historians record the Inca people as simple and uneducated based upon their presuppositions rooted in evolutionary philosophy which dictates a simple man evolving into a more scientifically cable man. To criticize the ethic and religion of the Incas would require acknowledging a standard that transcends human perspective—an absolute standard—like the standard revealed in the Bible. To reveal a transcendent standard is to acknowledge a transcendent Law Giver—God Himself. And to acknowledge an "advanced" and intelligent mankind prior to the evolutionary model's introduction of such "progression" is to acknowledge a faulty timeline at best, and a faulty system in its entirety at worst. If man was created, then he did not evolve. If man did not evolve, then evolutionists must abandon their religion of evolutionism!

# Question 2

A. Built in a location that naturally made their city more easily defendable from enemies.

B. Tight seams between huge slabs.

C. Slabs that had handles so they could be moved into place, and then later sanded off to make the stones smooth.

D. Specially designed seams between giant stones that acted as protection against earthquakes.

E. Left-over cylinders that may have been used in conjunction with levers that would possibly allow an individual to move incredibly heavy stones into place.

F. A complex series of drainage systems that allowed the inhabitants to have clean homes.

G. Temples in which the sun and moon shine through narrow holes in the rocks during special dates of the year.

H. Windows in buildings that line up with the surrounding mountains in which they worshipped.

# Question 3

A. God's ethic, as revealed to the children of Israel, includes the following: Deuteronomy 11:26-28 says, "Behold, I set before you today a blessing and a curse: the blessing, if you obey the commandments of the LORD your God which I command you today; and the curse, if you do not obey the commandments of the LORD your God, but turn aside from the way which I command you today, to go after other gods which you have not known." Civilizations rise and fall at God's pleasure. Examples of judgments and consequences are revealed in Leviticus 26 and Deuteronomy 28. As Egypt, Assyria, and Babylon were used to bring affliction upon Israel, so the Spaniards were used to bring to naught the once great Inca Empire.

# Question 4

A. Huáscar and Atahualpa engaged in a series of battles with tens of thousands of soldiers under their respective commands. Their rivalry severely weakened their strength at the time of the Spanish conquistadors' arrival. If the two brothers had been united in strength, they might have made a better stand against their enemies.

# Question 5

A. God is sovereign through all the events of history, and often raises up imperfect, sinful people to execute judgment on the sins of another nation. Victory of one nation over another does not mean that one was righteous and the other wicked. Read the book of Habakkuk, and see how Habakkuk struggled with the question of why the wicked nation of Babylon could be used to overthrow the nation of Israel. God responds in Habakkuk 1:5-7: "Behold ye among the heathen, and regard, and wonder marvelously: for I will work a work in your days, which ye will not believe, though it be told you. For, lo, I raise up the Chaldeans, that bitter and hasty nation, which shall march through the breadth of the land, to possess the dwelling places that are not theirs. They are terrible and dreadful: their judgment and their dignity shall proceed of themselves."

# Question 6

A. When a nation that believes their human leader is divine witnesses the frailty of their leader they are forced to see the frailty of their "god." They put their trust in a false god who is fallen, full of error, weak, and practices idolatry. When their human deity is proven to be only flesh, their religious fabric is destroyed, their god is exposed as a fraud, and they are left hopeless and in need of true spiritual reformation and the gospel.

B. Emperor Hirohito was supposedly the descendant of the "sun god." After Japan's defeat he admitted that he was not divine—he was only a man.

C. The people of the Incas thought that their leaders were also divine. Their own demise at the hands of an inferior number revealed their "divine" priests were false prophets. The Inca people were confronted with the bankruptcy of their false worship.

# Question 7

A. As a culture begins to reject the truth of creation, the Creator, God's Law, and His dominion mandate which sets men above the animals, they worship the creature rather than the Creator. Cultures degenerate and supplant anything and everything in the place of the Divine Creator and His will. As America's Christian culture erodes, many incorporate the old paganism as a "noble" tribal expression of their worship of the earth, their own will, and their rebellion against the commands of God. Many Christians excuse pagan practices, which include scarification and tattoos, suggesting that these practices can be "redeemed." However, our understanding of such practices should be governed by the word of God and our commitment to take every thought captive to the obedience of Christ. We must be transformed by the renewing of our minds, and come out from among the lost culture of this world to be separate and distinct through the practices and commands given by our God (Leviticus 19:28; Deuteronomy 14:1; Romans 12:2; 1 Corinthians 6:19-20)!

B. This compromise is the logical progression as a society rejects the One true God and worships creation rather than the Creator (Romans 1).

# Question 8

A. A grandfather cultivated a love for discipleship and exploration and taught his children the same. Hiram Bingham III stood on the shoulders of two great Christian Hiram Binghams. He was the grandson of the famous missionaries who helped convert the Hawaiian Islands to Jesus Christ, and the son of a famous father who went to the South Pacific and led islanders to the Lord. Later he would become the father of seven sons, including Hiram Bingham IV, who served as a diplomat and a spy, saving the lives of many Jews against the Nazi holocaust during the Second World War.

B. The Bingham family is a great testimony to Christian men discipling their children and exploring their world for the glory of Christ!

# Question 9

A. As a student, and later as a professor at Yale University, Bingham studied the history of the Incas. Fascinated by the stories of the last two missing Inca capitals, Vilcabamba and Vitcos, Bingham set out in 1911 with a small expeditionary force. He was a student of the Inca culture, and he was eager to discover what had been allusive for so long.

B. Bingham was lead to Machu Picchu by locals that were living in the surrounding area.

# Question 10

A. Machu Picchu was a spiritual and governmental seat in the great Inca Empire.

B. The leaders were the Inca priests, who led the rest of the population in pagan worship and human sacrifice. Their economy was agricultural.